The Dahlgren Affair: The History of the Civil War's Most Controversial Cavalry Raid

By Sean McLachlan and Charles River Editors

Dahlgren

About Charles River Editors

Charles River Editors provides superior editing and original writing services across the digital publishing industry, with the expertise to create digital content for publishers across a vast range of subject matter. In addition to providing original digital content for third party publishers, we also republish civilization's greatest literary works, bringing them to new generations of readers via ebooks.

Sign up here to receive updates about free books as we publish them, and visit Our Kindle Author Page to browse today's free promotions and our most recently published Kindle titles.

About the Author

Sean McLachlan is an author and historian. He has written numerous books and articles on military history as well as several works of fiction, including the Civil War novel *A Fine Likeness* and the *Trench Raiders* series World War One action novels. Feel free to visit him on his Amazon page and blog.

Introduction

The Dahlgren Affair

"Judson Kilpatrick, Ulric Dahlgren, and their probable patron Edwin Stanton set out to engineer the death of the Confederacy's president; the legacy spawned out of the utter failure of their effort may have included the death of their own president." – Stephen Sears, Civil War historian

Failing to secure the capture of any major northern cities, or the recognition of Great Britain or France, or the complete destruction of any northern armies, the Confederacy's last chance to survive the Civil War was the election of 1864. Democrats had been pushing an anti-war stance or at least a stance calling for a negotiated peace for years, so the South hoped that if a Democrat defeated President Lincoln, or if anti-war Democrats could retake the Congress, the North might negotiate peace with the South. In the election of 1862, anti-war Democrats made some gains in Congress and won the governorship of the State of New York. Confederates were therefore hopeful that trend would continue to the election of 1864.

It's now often forgotten that Lincoln's reelection was far from a foregone conclusion, and the fighting in 1864 would be desperate in both the East and West. The Overland Campaign that Ulysses S. Grant launched against Robert E. Lee's Army of Northern Virginia would be an extremely costly stalemate, so Lincoln's fate may have rested in the hands of William Tecumseh Sherman, whose successful Atlanta campaign shortly before the election may have been the decider. Sherman would spend the rest of the year on his infamous March to the Sea, laying waste to wide swathes of Georgia.

As controversial as the Overland Campaign and the March to the Sea were, however, the most controversial event of that year took place before either campaign. In March, skirmishing between the two sides' cavalry outside of Richmond left one 21 year old Union colonel, Ulric Dahlgren, dead, and when a young Virginian went through the items on his body, the orders that were found seemed almost too unbelievable to be true: "The men must keep together and well in hand, and once in the city it must be destroyed and Jeff. Davis and Cabinet killed."

When the papers on Dahlgren's body made their way to Confederate officials, the leaders decided to publicize them, leading officials in the North to denounce the papers as forgeries. Over 150 years later, the authenticity of the papers is still widely debated among historians. While most in the North dismissed the papers (and Dahlgren's father would work to clear his son's name for the rest of his own life), Union General George Meade questioned Judson Kilpatrick, the cavalry commander in charge of the raid, and he came away with the belief that at the very least, Kilpatrick had signed off on the conspiracy to assassinate the Confederate leadership. Nonetheless, he relayed to Lee that "neither the United States Government, myself, nor General Kilpatrick authorized, sanctioned, or approved the burning of the city of Richmond and the killing of Mr. Davis and cabinet."

Although it still remains one of the Civil War's most enduring mysteries, modern historians now mostly believe the orders were authentic, and that the responsibility for the plan may go all the way up to Secretary of War Edwin Stanton. Moreover, some of them, including noted historian Stephen Sears, believe that the Dahlgren Affair may have been one of the primary reasons John Wilkes Booth devised his own conspiracy to assassinate President Lincoln. That conspiracy, of course, would be far more successful than Dahlgren's.

The Dahlgren Affair: The History of the Civil War's Most Controversial Cavalry Raid chronicles the history and mystery of the conspiracy to kill the Confederacy's top leaders. Along with pictures of important people, places, and events, you will learn about the Dahlgren Affair like never before, in no time at all.

Chapter 1: The Context

By 1864, Ulysses S. Grant had already succeeded in achieving two of President Lincoln's three primary directives for a Union victory: the opening of the Mississippi Valley Basin, and the domination of the corridor from Nashville to Atlanta. If he could now seize Richmond, he would achieve the third.

However, even before beginning the Overland Campaign against Robert E. Lee's Army of Northern Virginia, Grant, Sherman and Lincoln devised a new strategy that would eventually implement total war tactics. Grant aimed to use the Army of the Potomac to attack Lee and/or take Richmond. Meanwhile, General Sherman, now in command of the Department of the West, would attempt to take Atlanta and strike through Georgia. In essence, having already cut the Confederacy in half with Vicksburg campaign, he now intended to bisect the eastern half.

On top of all that, Grant and Sherman were now intent on fully depriving the Confederacy of the ability to keep fighting. Sherman put this policy in effect during his March to the Sea by confiscating civilian resources and literally taking the fight to the Southern people. For Grant, it meant a war of attrition that would steadily bleed Lee's Army of Northern Virginia. To take full advantage of the North's manpower, in 1864 the Union also ended prisoner exchanges to ensure that the Confederate armies could not be bolstered by paroled prisoners.

"The Peacemakers," a painting depicting Lincoln, Grant, Sherman, and Admiral Porter

Thus, by 1864, things were looking so bleak for the South that the Confederate war strategy was simply to ensure Lincoln lost reelection that November, with the hope that a new Democratic president would end the war and recognize the South's independence. At the same time, the end of the prisoner exchanges compelled the South to build a large prison camp such as the one at Andersonville.

Even before the policy change, the prisoner exchange, which had flourished during the early years of the war, was complicated. Though it's hard to imagine today, the two sides used a parole system by which prisoners were let go after promising not to rejoin the fighting until they had officially been exchanged. Still, there were problems inherent in the system. For example, the sides had to determine how many privates were equal to an officer; for example, several privates were to be exchanged for one officer, and the higher the officer's rank, the more enlisted men had to be sacrificed.

Moreover, the South did not recognize black Union soldiers as real soldiers but instead saw them as "rebel slaves. It reached the point that the Union threatened to summarily execute Confederate prisoners if black soldiers weren't treated as normal prisoners, and the death knell of the prisoner exchange came in the wake of the Fort Pillow Massacre in April 1864.

Confederate cavalry commander Nathan Bedford Forrest already had a controversial Civil War record entering 1864, but he was about to participate in perhaps the most controversial battle of the war. After functioning as an independent raider for the next several months, on April 12, 1864, units of Forrest's cavalry surrounded Fort Pillow on the Mississippi River, north of Memphis. Ironically, the fort had been built in 1861 and named after General Gideon Pillow, the same General Pillow who proved wildly incompetent at Fort Donelson and ignored Forrest's suggestion to escape the siege instead of surrendering to Grant.

Forrest

As far as skirmishes go, Fort Pillow was a completely unremarkable fight. Before attacking, Forrest demanded the unconditional surrender of the Union garrison, a normal custom of his, and he warned the Union commanding officer that he would not be responsible for his soldiers' actions if the warning went unheeded. What made Fort Pillow markedly different was that a sizable amount of the Union garrison defending the Fort was comprised of black soldiers, which particularly enraged Confederate soldiers whenever they encountered those they viewed as former slaves in the field.

It is still unclear exactly how the fighting unfolded, but what is clear is that an unusually high percentage of Union soldiers were killed, and the Confederates were accused of massacring black soldiers after they had surrendered. Primary sources tell conflicting accounts of what happened at Battle of Fort Pillow, leaving scholars to piece together the battle and determine whether Confederate soldiers purposely shot Union soldiers after they had surrendered..

By May 1864, the Fort Pillow affair became a matter of Congressional investigations, with many leaders from both Union and Confederate camps anxious to condemn Forrest simply on principle alone.

Regardless, Fort Pillow permanently marred Forrest's reputation for the rest of his life, and it was featured prominently in his obituaries throughout the North in 1877. It was also responsible for the primary breakdown of the exchanges, and with that, prisons on both sides were allowed to profligate and grow.

As a result, prisons in the South were becoming overcrowded. The Confederacy had little food or medicine to spare and prisoners of war found themselves barely able to survive. One of the worst was Libby Prison in Richmond, where large numbers of men died each month from disease, malnutrition, and exposure. The prison was a converted warehouse owned by ship chandlers Libby and Son. At first it had been reserved for officers who could expect to be exchanged in a month or less, but as the prisoner exchange system fell apart, the prison population swelled and overcrowding became rife.

In February of 1864, a group of Union officers tunneled out of Libby Prison in the war's most remarkable jailbreak. Colonel Thomas Rose of the 77th Pennsylvania Volunteers led a team that cut through a basement foundation wall and excavated a tunnel almost sixty feet long to emerge inside a tobacco shed. 109 men managed to sneak out, slipping through Confederate lines and made it safely back to the Union, where they spread the word about the sufferings of their fellow prisoners. The press went wild with the story, printing page after page of grim details about prison life. The public demanded that something be done.

Chapter 2: The Plan

With the understandable furor that conditions at Confederate prisons caused in the North, efforts were quickly made to do something about the most notorious camps, including Libby Prison in Richmond and Andersonville in Georgia. In early 1864, Major General Benjamin Butler suggested a cavalry raid from his position at Fort Monroe at the tip of the Virginia Peninsula. The raid would strike at Richmond, cause as much havoc as possible, and release the men incarcerated at Libby Prison. He also planned to hit the Tredegar Iron Works, one of the last major factories left to the Confederacy. Butler even hoped to capture Confederate President Jefferson Davis.

Butler

It was a bold plan, but it quickly fell apart thanks to poor security. A Union deserter told the Confederates of the raid and on February 7, 1864, just as Butler's column was getting underway, rebel forces under General Eppa Hunton stopped it in its tracks at Bottoms Bridge. Without the element of surprise, there could be no hope for success and the raiders turned back to Fort Monroe, leaving Hunton to wonder what the purpose of the raid had been.

Naturally, the idea of freeing the prisoners did not die with Butler's raid, and less than a week later Brigadier General Hugh Judson Kilpatrick proposed another raid with the same goals. Kilpatrick was only 26, young for a general, and his ambition knew no bounds. He saw his military service as a step towards political advancement. Kilpatrick had it all planned out. First he would ride to glory during the war. Then he would go back to his native state of New Jersey and run for governor. After that, who knew? Perhaps he would make a bid for the White House. But first he needed to secure his fame on the battlefield. He had no doubt that he would do so.

Kilpatrick

Perhaps not surprisingly, overconfidence was his fatal flaw. Kilpatrick had earned the nickname "Kill Cavalry" for his habit of driving men and mounts past the limits of endurance. His units tended to suffer high casualties in battle thanks to his habit of taking risks. That said, while his men may have grumbled, they had to acknowledge that Kilpatrick never asked them to do anything he wasn't willing to do himself; Kilpatrick led from the front with reckless abandon, and earned a great deal of respect for doing so. He had even earned a modest amount of fame for being the first Regular army officer to be wounded in action when he got shot at the Battle of Big Bethel, one of the earliest engagements of the war, on June 10, 1861. He quickly rose in the ranks as a "fighting officer" at a time when the politicians and the public were frustrated by many officers and political generals who seemed too cautious in the face of the enemy. Kilpatrick, however, could have used a bit more caution. At times he behaved erratically under pressure, losing his head in battle and not thinking clearly. This flaw was overlooked by his superiors.

Driven, arrogant, and completely convinced of his own worth, Kilpatrick was not a man to be stopped. He showed a great deal of self-discipline in some areas of his life—a willingness to ride on grueling cavalry raids, and an aversion to drink and gambling that was unusual at that time. He did have one vice, however; he was a notorious womanizer, despite being married. Perhaps it suited his vanity to attract women, or perhaps romantic conquests were just another goal to be achieved. While he never got in official trouble for the many women of questionable virtue who could be found in his camp, he did have two brushes with military authorities, once when he was accused of selling captured Confederate goods for his own profit and again when he was accused of accepting bribes. Both times he was able to use his political connections to emerge from scandal unscathed. The army needed fighting men, and Kilpatrick, whatever his flaws may have been, certainly proved he was one of those.

The previous year during the Chancellorsville Campaign, Major General George Stoneman had sent Kilpatrick on a cavalry raid aimed at cutting the railroad lines from Richmond that supplied General Lee's army. It was hoped that this would distract Lee from the real intentions of the campaign.

Stoneman

The raid failed to distract Lee, and the lack of cavalry led directly to the success of Stonewall Jackson's legendary flank attack and the Army of the Potomac's disastrous loss, but it caught the imagination of many in the Union command. Kilpatrick led his men around Lee's army, burning railroads, mills, and bridges, and made it almost to the outskirts of the city. Stoneman's Raid, as it came to be called, showed that while Lee could intercept the movements of a large army, a smaller raiding force could slip by him and strike at the very nerve center of the Confederacy.

By March 1864, Kilpatrick was in command of the Third Division of the Army of the Potomac's Cavalry Corps. While his star had risen high, it had recently become rather tarnished. At a late stage of the Battle of Gettysburg in 1863, he was frustrated that he had been kept out of the fighting and ordered a suicidal charge against an entrenched rebel position, losing many men in the process. The following months did not provide him with an opportunity to redeem himself and his critics began to talk openly of their distaste for this impulsive braggart. However, despite these setbacks, he was in a position to make his opinions heard. A raid to free the prisoners would not only buoy up the morale of the war-weary North, it would reinvigorate his career.

Using his contacts within the Republican Party, Kilpatrick managed to arrange a meeting with Lincoln on February 12, 1864, and outlined his plan. The fact that he didn't go through regular military channels to secure the meeting was yet another indication of Kilpatrick's overeager nature, but Lincoln listened to the general's plans with interest and approved of a raid to free the prisoners at Libby, destroy the railroad, and distribute an amnesty proclamation open to anyone who swore allegiance to the United States. The previous year, after the failed Stoneman's Raid, the president felt that a major opportunity had been missed; other than Lee's large army looming nearby, the capital itself was only lightly defended by militia and home guards who had little or no battlefield experience. Their ranks were made up of older men and teenage boys, or those who were not healthy enough to march with the field army. While decently armed, they were strung out to protect various fords, roads, the railway, and important buildings such as mills. They would have difficulty uniting these scattered forces because few of them had horses or mules. The Confederate army, chronically short of mounts, could spare few for these reserve troops. They were also short on artillery. At the time of the previous raid, Lincoln had stated that the raiders "could have safely gone in and burnt everything and brought us Jeff Davis."

For this raid, however, Lincoln did not consider the Confederate president to be on the agenda. Kilpatrick was sent to Secretary of War Edwin Stanton to work out the details of the raid, and there is no mention in their plans of capturing Davis or any other politician.

Stanton

Kilpatrick was obliged to put his plan on paper for the study of the high command. In a letter dating February 17, he wrote:

> "I propose, with a force of not less than 4,000 cavalry and six guns, to cross the Rapidan River at Ely's Ford and proceed to Spotsylvania Court House, from that point to send a sufficient force of cavalry to destroy the Virginia Central Railroad at or near Frederick's Hall, to prevent infantry reinforcements being sent from Lee's army, scouts having been sent to cut the telegraph on crossing the Rapidan River; also to send a force to destroy the Fredericksburg railroad at or near Guiney's Station, the telegraph on this road having also been previously destroyed. These parties, and others that it may be found necessary to detach, will scatter the proclamation along the line of march. With the main force I propose to move to Carmel Church and cross the North Anna River near that point, destroy the railroad bridge three miles below, and proceed to Hanover Junction, unless the force stationed there is found to be too large, in which case I will avoid that point. The force sent to Guiney's Station will join me at Carmel Church. The force sent to Frederick's Hall will proceed to Goochland Court-House, destroy the canal, cross the James River, proceed down the south bank, destroy the arsenal at Bellona; also the Danville and Richmond and Petersburg and Richmond Railroads, this force afterward to act as circumstances may require. From Hanover Junction I will proceed down the Brook pike between the two railroads, cross the brook and move on Richmond, and if possible, in conjunction with troops sent from the direction of West Point, make an attempt to release our prisoners. Should this be found impossible, the command can return by way of Fredericksburg, or seek temporary safety at West Point. The command will need but five days rations and one of forage; no wagons.

> "From the information I have but lately received, and from my thorough knowledge of the country, I am satisfied that this plan can be safely and successfully carried out."

The first opposition to the plan came from the high command of the Army of the Potomac. Major General George Meade had serious doubts about the plan in general and Kilpatrick in particular, but since both Lincoln and Stanton had already given their stamp of approval, he kept his opinions to himself. Meade washed his hands of the affair by telling Kilpatrick, "No detailed instructions are given you, since the plan of your operations has been proposed by yourself, with the sanction of the President and the Secretary of War…" But in a letter to his wife, Meade revealed his true thoughts. "The undertaking is a desperate one, but the anxiety and distress of the public and of the authorities at Washington is so great that it seems to demand running great risks for the chances of success."

Meade

For his part, Major General Alfred Pleasonton, commanding the cavalry corps, did not keep quiet. In a letter to Major-General Humphreys, the Chief of Staff of the Army of the Potomac, dated February 17, Pleasanton wrote:

"The plan proposed by Brigadier-General Kilpatrick in the enclosed communication is not feasible at this time. When the Stoneman raid was made last year, General Lee's army was closely engaged with the Army of the Potomac at Chancellorsville, and the country was clear, yet the damage done by that raid was repaired in a few days, while the loss to the Government was over 7,000 horses, besides the equipment and men left on the road. Had this force been retained for the Gettysburg campaign, the results would have been more decisive.

"General Kilpatrick might succeed in cutting the telegraph from Lee's army and from Fredericksburg to Richmond, but the telegraph by the way of Gordonsville and Lynchburg would soon notify the rebels in Richmond that our cavalry was out, and before Kilpatrick could do much damage, their vulnerable points would be secured. For the success of such an expedition I would be willing to sacrifice the number of horses required, but in the present state of the roads and the facilities the rebels have, with their army disengaged and distributed for frustrating such an effort, I cannot recommend it.

"In reference to the President's proclamation, I will most willingly undertake to have it freely circulated in any section of Virginia that may be desired. I do not think I am promising too much in naming even Richmond.

"I am in the receipt of information from the James River which is satisfactory to me that the amnesty proclamation is freely circulating in Virginia, but that the people are so watched as to prevent much action as yet on their part. As an instance is mentioned a strong Union man at Howardsville, who has $160,000 in coin secreted, but who has never been able to escape with it."

Pleasonton's concerns were noted but his objection was overruled.

Pleasonton

The plan was simple and daring. Kilpatrick's cavalry would move out from their camp near Stevensburg and Culpepper, riding hard for Richmond 70 miles to the southeast. For the sake of speed, there would be no wagons. They would cross the Rapidan River and move to the Spotsylvania Court House, where the column would split. Two detachments would destroy portions of the Virginia Central and Richmond Railroad and the Fredericksburg and Potomac Railroad. The main body would ride straight for the city, crossing the North Anna River. One of the detachments would catch up with the main body as it continued towards the city destroying the depot and railroad bridge at Hanover Junction.

The other detachment, numbering about 500 men, would skirt Richmond to the west to fall upon the city from the south, where the defenses were even lighter. There was little danger from Lee's Army of Northern Virginia, which was positioned well north of the city bracing itself for movement across the Rapidan and Rappahannock Rivers by the Army of the Potomac, much like the year before. Thus, Richmond might be caught in a pincer movement, its infrastructure destroyed and its prisoners freed before Lee could respond. Moreover, Lee's army would be distracted by a feint that included cavalry led by a dashing young cavalry officer named George Armstrong Custer. Once the city was struck, the raiders would reunite and head back north, or if circumstances dictated, they would head down the Virginia Peninsula to the safety of Butler's lines.

Thus, the raiders expected little resistance. The city itself was defended by only about 3,000 militia and a small number of cavalry. The only regular troops nearby were 1,500 somewhat dispersed men under Major General Wade Hampton III. Even if this force could unite and move quickly enough to engage the raiders, they would be badly outnumbered.

Foolishly, Kilpatrick was busy bragging about his upcoming raid to anyone who would listen, and with that, what should have been a secret plan to catch the Confederacy by surprise was soon the talk of Washington. It wasn't long before the Northern papers reported on the raid, even preparing maps of its likely route. The Southern papers picked up on this news and began to report it as well.

Word of the raid soon reached the ears of Colonel Ulric Dahlgren, an eager 21 year old cavalry officer who, despite having lost his right leg below the knee, wanted to join in the fun. He hobbled into Kilpatrick's office one day, his wooden leg thumping on the ground, and begged to be allowed to ride into Richmond with him.

Dahlgren had made a name for himself as a daring, young officer. Being the son of Rear Admiral John Dahlgren, he had access far beyond that of a regular colonel. Lincoln himself had signed his commission at the beginning of the war. Kilpatrick was impressed with the fiery young man and decided, despite his infirmity that left him needing a pair of canes in order to walk and the fact that the two hadn't worked together before, to put him in command of the smaller of the two wings, the one that would ride around Richmond and attack from the south. Dahlgren was given the trickiest job in the raid despite never having led one before, no doubt due in large part to the fact that Kilpatrick also saw in Dahlgren's impetuous actions proof that he would be willing to go beyond the rules of civilized warfare.

John Dahlgren

Dahlgren was overjoyed at the trust Kilpatrick placed in him. The young man had been depressed since poor medical treatment after getting wounded near Gettysburg had left him with an infection that required amputation. For months he had languished on one of his father's ships, slowly recovering and wondering if he would ever fight again. Now he had his chance, and what a chance it was. He wrote his father, "There is a grand raid to be made, and I am to have a very important command. If successful, it will be the grandest thing on record; and if it fails, many of us will 'go up'…but it is an undertaking that if I were not in, I should be ashamed to show my face again."

As bold as the raid was, it did not go ahead without careful planning. The troopers and their horses were vetted to make sure everyone was in the best of health, and only the finest of each were picked from several regiments. Weapons and equipment were checked, and the routes and targets discussed in detail. A trooper in the 17th Pennsylvania who would ride in the raid wrote about the preparations, "Five days' rations of hard bread, sugar, coffee and salt were issued, but no meat, the command evidently being supposed to furnish meat for itself from some source other than Uncle Sam's commissary. This looked extremely raidish. Commanding officers of detachments were ordered to see that all horses were well shod, inspection of arms and ammunition, everything in the best condition possible. . . Everybody was in excellent humor, for nothing so delights the heart of a cavalryman as to go on a scout or a raid. It is easier to get a trooper or even a hundred for a raid than to get one to groom an extra horse."

Kilpatrick conferred with the Bureau of Military Information about the latest intelligence reports from spies within the Confederate lines, gaining valuable information about road conditions and the positions and numbers of the city's defenders. The Bureau also provided several of its own men, led by Captain John McEntee, to ride with the Dahlgren wing of the raid. The young colonel would be going deep into enemy territory and would need someone who was familiar with the ground. Kilpatrick would need no such assistance, since he was riding much the same route that he had nine months previously on the Stoneman Raid.

Chapter 3: The Raid

Kilpatrick received his official orders on February 27, but these were little more than authorization to do what he wished. No detailed plans were contained within the orders and Kilpatrick was left with a free hand. This also left him with full responsibility, something Meade and Pleasonton wished for him and not for themselves.

On February 28, Kilpatrick and Dahlgren set out just after dusk with about 3,800 men across the Rapidan River around Lee's right flank. In the meantime, Meade's army launched a three-pronged diversion on Lee's left. This diversion included 1,500 cavalrymen under Brigadier General George Armstrong Custer, plus a large number of infantry bringing with them wagons, artillery, and ambulances to make it look like the vanguard of the main army. As expected, this got the attention of General Lee, who shifted some regiments to deal with the threat.

Custer and Pleasonton in 1863

Custer's official report, dated March 1, demonstrated his famous love of adventure and supreme self-confidence: "I have just arrived at this point with my entire command. I will send a full report of my operations. My command is now being fed. I will probably return to Culpeper tonight. My horses are very much worn. I found Charlottesville and the bridge over the Rivanna [River] guarded by four batteries of artillery, two brigades of cavalry, and a very large force of infantry. This will be sufficient reason for my not having destroyed the railroad bridge, but I destroyed the fine frame bridge over that stream, within two miles of the railroad; captured and destroyed a large camp of the enemy, after driving them from it; captured six caissons loaded with ammunition, two forges, and harness for both caissons and forges; burnt three large flouring mills filled with grain; captured one standard bearing the Virginia State arms; captured about 500 horses, two Government wagons, one loaded with bacon, and on my return was cut off by a large force of cavalry and artillery under Generals Stuart and Wickham. My command cut its way through without losing a man, except a few wounded. The enemy had several killed, a large number wounded, and we captured over 50 prisoners. Since yesterday morning I have marched 100 miles." He later related that he had come away with about 500 horses and that more than a hundred runaway slaves joined the column and made it to the North.

Dahlgren's force set out at about 6 p.m., with Kilpatrick's larger column waiting for an hour more in order not to clog up the road. The weather was foggy, perfect for keeping a belated cloak of secrecy over the raid but making it difficult for the signalers to maintain communication between the different detachments. Thanks to the fog, Dahlgren's advance guard secured the ford over the Rapidan River, capturing 17 rebel guards without firing a shot or raising an alarm.

Dahlgren's force did, however, get spotted by a pair of General Hampton's scouts dressed in captured Union uniforms. In the dim moonlight the rebels were able to slip into the column and ride with the troopers, listening to their every word. After counting the number of men and getting a fair idea of their intentions, they disappeared into the night and galloped off to warn General Hampton.

Hampton III

The following morning, the column took separate roads just past Spotsylvania. Dahlgren set out with 460 men to make a wide circle around Richmond to the west and hit it from the south, where its defenses were at their weakest. The remainder of the force stayed with Kilpatrick, who would launch a simultaneous attack on the city from the north. Kilpatrick hoped to divert the defenders' attention so that Dahlgren would face little or no opposition. Both sections of the raid were supposed to attack Richmond at 10 a.m. on March 1, and once they freed the prisoners, the two wings would hopefully meet and withdraw to the safety of Union lines.

It was now February 29th (it being a leap year) and Dahlgren rode for his first major objective: Frederick's Hall, a depot on the Virginia Central Railway. Military Intelligence reported that Lee's Second Corps artillery was being stored there under a light guard. If these guns could be destroyed, it would be a major blow for the Army of Northern Virginia, which was already short of artillery.

As he approached the depot, he captured a group of Confederate officers engaged in court martial proceedings. Dahlgren questioned them about what lay ahead, and they told him the depot was heavily defended. At first Dahlgren thought they were just trying to scare him, but an old slave from a nearby plantation told him the same thing. Thus, decided to press ahead to his primary objective and avoid the depot.

As it turned out, Dahlgren missed a golden opportunity. The slave didn't know what he was talking about, and the Confederate officers had indeed been lying. In fact, the depot only had a few defenders that Dahlgren's force could have easily brushed aside, and furthermore, a train was just passing through carrying Robert E. Lee from Richmond back to his field headquarters. Dahlgren could have simultaneously decapitated and crippled the Army of Northern Virginia.

Meanwhile, Kilpatrick's column crossed the Po River and ate a hurried breakfast. They were so hurried, in fact, that many men grumbled they hadn't had time to eat. "Kill Cavalry" didn't give his men much rest even on a normal day, and today he was riding to glory. As they continued their ride, they tore down telegraph lines while meeting little resistance. Nevertheless, Kilpatrick was worried about what was happening with Dahlgren's wing of the raid. The land Kilpatrick was riding through was flat and wooded, and his signals officer could find no vantage point from which to communicate with his counterpart in Dahlgren's group. Soon it began to snow heavily, cutting down visibility even more. From then on, the two leaders would be on their own.

By noon, Confederate General Hampton had learned of the movements of both sections of the raid. The Confederate scouts who had ridden with Dahlgren for a time had arrived at his headquarters and given a full report, and another scout had reported on Kilpatrick's force. Hampton sent word to Confederate cavalry leader J.E.B. Stuart, but upon receiving no immediate reply he sent out what few men he could spare from his small and rather dispersed force. He ordered 300 cavalry and two cannons down the Richmond, Fredericksburg & Potomac Railroad. He also sent word to a cavalry brigade under Colonel Bradley Johnson at Taylorsville to chase the raiders.

These few forces would be badly outnumbered, but there was nothing more Hampton could do. The Confederates would have some trouble finding them. The snow was coming down quickly, making it hard for anyone to find their way and covering the tracks of those who had gone before. This helped Kilpatrick in another way. He was able to ride into Beaver Dam train station unnoticed, surprising the telegraph officer and capturing him before he could raise the alarm.

Kilpatrick's men set about burning the depot, warming themselves by the rising flames and celebrating this easy victory. Morale soared as the men hoped the snowstorm would hide their movements all the way to Richmond. One trooper wrote, "The dark forms of our soldiers jumping and dancing around. . .seemed from a distance like demons on some hellish sport."

In fact, the real "hellish sport" came soon enough. Local militia had seen the flames and as the column continued down the road they were harassed by sniper fire. The snipers were few and strung out along several miles, but that only added to the tension. The cavalry never knew when the next bullet would come snapping out of the snowstorm from an unseen gunman.

The column forged ahead. At the town of Ashland, Kilpatrick questioned some locals who claimed that 2,000 infantry, supported by artillery, were guarding a nearby railroad bridge. Kilpatrick didn't have to cross their path, but he didn't want such a force on his flank or rear either, so he sent 450 of his men under Major Hall to pin down the rebels at the bridge while he continued on with the mission. Just as with the report that spooked Dahlgren, this one was highly exaggerated and Kilpatrick need not have worried. Major Hall did meet resistance on the bridge from a force that included artillery, but they were easily beaten. In his official report, Kilpatrick claimed that the brief fight "deceived the enemy as to the movements of the main column." That may have been so, but it also alerted everyone in the vicinity that there was a raid on.

The snowfall slowed Kilpatrick down and he was still five miles from Richmond at 10 a.m. on March 1, the time for both wings to strike. It turned to an icy rain, soaking the raiders but not damping Kilpatrick's spirit. However, two miles further on, the raiders were shocked when they came upon hastily built earthworks on both sides of the road; Hampton had alerted the home guards and now the rebel militia opened fire with rifles and artillery. Within minutes, Kilpatrick lost dozens of men.

The resistance was too stiff to simply ride through, and fearing he faced veteran troops instead of the city militia, Kilpatrick dismounted and deployed his troops. The fighting intensified, and yet he did not deploy his own artillery because there was no cover for them. With such a deadly fire coming from the earthworks, his crew would be picked off before they could load. He also found that his troopers' carbines and pistols were no match for rifles and cannon.

Despite the resistance, the prize was too close to give up, so Kilpatrick's men kept at it, maintaining a steady fire on the defenders and trying to advance on the earthwork. The defenders stuck fast, and the fight stretched on into the afternoon. Kilpatrick's men slowly gained ground and the artillery was able to deploy in a protected position.

Kilpatrick regrouped and organized a two-pronged attack on the weakest part of the earthworks. Just as his men deployed, however, Kilpatrick had second thoughts. This was a weakness that had been apparent in his character in earlier battles; he would be bold and brash, but then suddenly lose heart. Kilpatrick later reported that he thought the defenders were being reinforced, but it isn't clear that this was so. Regardless, he decided to withdraw and ordered his men to head northwards, away from the city, away from the Union prisoners, and away from Dahlgren. In his report he said he felt sure Dahlgren had failed as well, although why he would think this when he hadn't heard from the man is unclear.

Either way, the column withdrew to Mechanicsville, where it was joined by the screening force that had been guarding against the defenders of the railroad bridge. Despite this reinforcement, and the fact that together they had captured some 200 prisoners, Kilpatrick did not have the nerve to go back on the attack. They settled in to cook some dinner and wait out the night.

Almost immediately, word of the raid had reached the prisoners at Libby. Lieutenant George Lodge of the 53rd Illinois Infantry, who kept a diary during his incarceration, had been a prisoner for almost nine months and the news rekindled his failing hopes. The Confederate reaction to the raid, however, made him fear for his life.

"Tuesday, March 1, 1864

"The Rebels have a terrific scare on today. Our cavalry are reported to be near the city again, and the Militia, Jack Ass Battery, etc., have all gone out. They have taken several prisoners this evening but do not let them come up among us. . .The nefarious order of the prison authorities to fire on any prisoner who put his head out of the window recoiled on themselves beautifully yesterday. The order is that if we hang clothes out of a window to dry, they will be confiscated; and if we sit in a window or lean against the iron gratings, we are liable to be shot. Yesterday a man in the deserters' Prison looked out of a window, and the guard shot him through the head, supposing him to be a Yankee; but he proved to have been a rebel detective officer who was on duty in the prison. I am sorry for the wife and three children he leaves.

"Wednesday, March 2, 1864

"Today they have done the most villainous thing of the war. Richard Turner, the Prison inspector, told Adjutant R. C. Knaggs that they had placed a mine of 300 pounds of Powder under the centre of this building so that if our cavalry were to come in, they could spring this mine and blow us into Eternity before we could be released."

While that sounded like a prison rumor or a scare put on the prisoners to keep them quiet, subsequent investigations revealed that the mining of the prison did indeed take place.

Later that night, Kilpatrick was feeling better. His scouts told him that instead of seasoned veterans, the defenders from the previous day were inexperienced militia. Even more, they had massed their scant numbers on that one road, thus leaving other approaches to the city lightly guarded or completely open. Thus, by midnight, his troopers were back on their horses and divided into two strike forces of 500 men each. A larger reserve force, led by himself and including the artillery, would act as rearguard while securing the bridge over the Chickahominy River. The reserve force would also guard the prisoners.

Naturally, the raiders were exhausted, having spent almost two days in almost constant riding and skirmishing. Some even nodded off in the saddle. Then, just as the troopers were setting off, the camp was thrown into chaos; General Hampton's veteran cavalry had arrived, riding through the camp and blasting at the Union troops at point blank range with their pistols. The fight raged in almost pitch darkness, with the Union raiders never seeing just how few enemies they faced.

Kilpatrick regrouped his men and fought back, but then Confederate artillery boomed out of the night. Now Kilpatrick gave up completely, and the brief rise in his hopes had vanished. He ordered his confused men to withdraw. Many got lost in the darkness and got killed or captured, while others wandered off in the wrong direction. The bulk, however, fell into line and soon found themselves riding in the direction of the Virginia Peninsula with Hampton's cavalry snapping at their heels. The raid was over, and the retreat had begun, at least for Kilpatrick's wing.

Shortly after sunup on March 2, Kilpatrick formed his men into a firing line ready to repulse the next attack by the rebel cavalry. By daylight Hampton's numbers were revealed to be much less than previously supposed. With renewed confidence the raiders stopped Hampton's attack dead in its tracks and forced the rebels to retreat, taking more prisoners. Kilpatrick reported, "This was the last I saw of the enemy. From the prisoners I learned that they belonged to Hampton's division, and that it was he who attacked me the night before; that he had with him a large force of mounted infantry and cavalry and four pieces of artillery, and that he had retired to Hanover Junction, expecting me to move in that direction. Taking this fact into consideration, and the condition of my command, I decided to move by the nearest route to General Butler's lines at New Kent Court-House. The command went into camp near Tunstall's Station Wednesday evening."

Kilpatrick's men had not pursued them far. Rest and food were more important and so they snatched a few peaceful hours to cook and sleep. The horses were fed and given some much-needed rest, but it is doubtful they were unsaddled. When an emergency could happen at any moment, a cavalryman kept his saddle tightened and ready, even if it made the horse suffer. Cavalry raids took a terrible toll on horses, and they would often need weeks of rest afterwards.

Kilpatrick ordered a roll call, and he found two officers and 50 men missing. The previous night had taken a heavy toll. In addition, the column had lost a hundred horses, bolted or shot in the surprise attack. Many of his men now rode double, and some nursed wounds that made it look unlikely they would ever see Union lines.

By early afternoon on March 2, Kilpatrick still had heard no word from Dahlgren. He had hoped a messenger would come through somehow, or at least to hear the sound of firing coming from the direction of the Confederate capital, but there was nothing. Kilpatrick was now despondent. He ordered his men to mount up and led the column towards the Virginia Peninsula. It soon met up with a force sent by General Butler to assist in their retreat. Kilpatrick could only hope that Dahlgren had succeeded somehow, and that the raid had not been a total failure.

As it turned out, Dahlgren had run into the same problems that had checked Kilpatrick. After shying away from attacking Frederick's Hall depot and missing his chance at the biggest coup of the war, he made his way towards the James River, distributing copies of Lincoln's amnesty proclamation to every civilian he passed and leaving them at every building. They also took the time to destroy important property such as mills and grain stores. Dahlgren's column swelled as runaway slaves riding their former masters' horses and mules joined with them, hoping for an armed escort to freedom.

Along the route he came to the house of Confederate Secretary of War James Seddon. The man wasn't in, but Mrs. Seddon received him and showed him remarkably polite hospitality considering the circumstances. Mrs. Seddon revealed that Dahlgren's father, now rear admiral in the hated Yankee Navy, had courted her many years before. Mrs. Seddon offered the younger Dahlgren a toast of blackberry wine for old time's sake, Dahlgren thanked her, and with a tip of his hat he went back to cutting his way through her country.

Seddon

On the afternoon of March 2, he at last reached the James River, which he should have reached hours before, but it made little difference. Jude's Ferry, which was supposed to be fordable, was swollen thanks to the recent weather. Dahlgren turned to his guide, a freedman named Martin Robinson, who had brought them to this spot with the assurance that it was fordable year round, and accused the black man of having tricked them. Putting common sense aside in favor of finding a scapegoat, he ordered Martin hanged. Dahlgren then led his men along the north bank, looking for a place to cross. On their way they continued to destroy any property of worth, anticipating Sherman's scorched earth policy during his March to the Sea later that year.

Dahlgren now resigned himself to not being able to circle the city and attack from the vulnerable southern roads because there simply wasn't time. He would instead attack from the west, and if the defenses were stronger there as the Union spies said, then he would just have to smash through them.

Even with the unwanted shortcut, the roads were so bad Dahlgren knew he wouldn't be able to attack the city until shortly before nightfall, so he sent a small group of couriers to give Kilpatrick the message, but they didn't get far before they were captured. As the snow continued to fall, Dahlgren's weary horsemen plodded on. There was a brief period of excitement when they heard distant sounds of battle. Kilpatrick, Dahlgren assumed, was making his move. The firing died out too quickly, however, and Dahlgren was left wondering if his commander had made it into the city or had been forced to retreat.

As the overcast sky darkened and foretold another chilly night, Dahlgren's men were suddenly jolted out of their lethargy by the sound of rifle fire; they had reached the outskirts of the city and been spotted by the militia. Dahlgren bellowed out the order to charge. If he didn't break through before dark, he would be stuck on the road until morning and would surely face heavy reinforcements. He led his men into the hail of bullets, saddles emptying to his left and right, and drove the militia two miles. Both sides suffered heavy casualties, but it was Dahlgren who lost his nerve. Suddenly there were mounted rebels in front of him. Thinking the Confederate reinforcements had arrived already, Dahlgren sounded the retreat.

Darkness fell and the column was able to disengage from the fight, get around the city, and head northeast towards the Pamunkey River. His troopers, now thoroughly exhausted, suffered through a long night. Freezing rain and snow drove down on them, and every now and then the darkness lit up with the rifle fire of hidden snipers.

Darkness and fatigue led to confusion, and about 300 men under Captain John Mitchell, 2nd New York Cavalry, ended up taking the wrong trail and got separated from the 80 or so men under Dahlgren. Mitchell crossed the Meadow Bridge over the Chickahominy River, fighting much of the way as they headed for an agreed-upon rendezvous in case of trouble: Tunstall's Station on the Richmond & York River Railroad. They found Kilpatrick there late on March 2 and joined them on their retreat to Fort Monroe. There seems to have been little attempt to discover Dahlgren's fate. They would later hear of it in the newspapers.

At some point in the night, Dahlgren became aware that he had lost most of his men. There was little he could do but hope to find them further down the road, and continued to the Chickahominy River, crossing at a point to the north of the bridge his subordinate had used. He then crossed the Pamunkey River near Hanover Town, heading north and east, seeking escape.

Richmond's defenders were now on full alert. Couriers galloped between isolated guard detachments, spreading the latest news. When units of Richmond's militia or an increasing number of regular units stopped to question local farmers and shopkeepers, the civilians pointed out which route the raiders had taken. Their testimony was supported by rebel soldiers who had managed to escape from the column, and from recaptured slaves who had left the raiders thinking they might have a better shot at freedom by going their own way. The rebels began to grow in numbers, closing in.

One contingent following Dahlgren's isolated force was Company H of the 9th Virginia Cavalry, led by Lieutenant James Pollard. He only had a couple of dozen men, but he wasn't about to let the Yankee raiders escape. With so many other units scouring the countryside, he hoped he would soon have a large enough force to whip the raiders.

A group of bushwhackers caught Dahlgren first, finding him and his men just as they were crossing the Mattaponi River, the horses swimming, small groups of the men taking turns to cross with a single rowboat. "Bushwhackers" had become a general term for guerrilla fighters, especially rebels, who fought the war "on their own hook." They were generally men of fighting age who decided not to join the regular army or militia and often only fought part time. They were especially common in Union-occupied border areas, especially Missouri and Kansas, but there were plenty around Virginia too.

When these citizen soldiers started firing at those raiders who remained on the near bank, they saw the incredible sight of a man with a wooden leg hobble into range, tuck his cane under his arm, and blast away at them with his pistol. After this show of defiance, Dahlgren reached the far shore uninjured, and Pollard and his men made it to the river shortly thereafter.

However, the Virginia cavalryman guessed the route that the raiders were heading and hurried through the woods and fields to cut them off. At the little village of Stevensville they gathered some more cavalry and a force of local militia, many of them schoolboys, led by their schoolmaster, Edward Halbach.

Pollard returned to the main road and found they had gotten ahead of Dahlgren. Hurriedly he deployed his men in the woods next to the road near Mantapike Hill, on the left bank of the Mattaponi River, and settled down to ambush the Federals.

Around 11:30 p.m. on March 2, Dahlgren rode straight into the Confederate ambush. As his diminished column approached Mantapike Hill, Dahlgren sensed there was something amiss. He ordered his men to halt and rode a little ahead on his own. Suddenly he spotted or heard movement in the nearby woods. He stood up in his stirrups and drew his revolver. Pointing it at the dimly seen tree line, he ordered, "Surrender, or I'll shoot!"

The only reply was silence. Perhaps the experienced rebel cavalry were waiting for the rest of the raiders to come closer, or perhaps the home guards were unsure what to do or were waiting for orders from Pollard. Whatever went through their minds, none squeezed the trigger. Dahlgren fired first, but instead of a loud bang all anyone heard was an ineffective click as the percussion cap turned out to be a dud. That sound was enough to galvanize the rebels into action, and a volley crashed through Dahlgren and raked down the Union column. Dahlgren and several others pitched from their saddles.

With that, Dahlgren's men broke. They had ridden too far, suffered too much, failed too badly, and now their officer lay slain. If they had kept their heads, they might have been able to push the rebels back; Pollard's regulars were still badly outnumbered and the rest of his little force were home guards, many of them mere schoolboys armed with shotguns, no match for rifles or carbines, which had better range. One veteran of the fight recalled that their ammunition was also poor. Even so, the rebels had the advantage of surprise and did not fire until the Union raiders were quite close.

As the rebels kept up the heavy fire, more raiders were knocked off their horses. Others ran off, joining the two remaining rebel prisoners and the escaped slaves in an all-out sprint for safety. A few tried to fight, but in the confusion many of them ended up being taken captive. One small group managed to break out. After a desperate ride they made it to Butler's lines and told of what had happened. Other Union raiders, bunched in a nearby field or scattered by ones and twos in the woods, gave themselves up. One Confederate veteran recalled, "It was a humiliated outfit when it was seen by how small a handful it had been captured, but it was too late."

Of Pollard's exploits, Major General J.E.B. Stuart wrote, "Lieutenant Pollard deserves great credit for his gallantry, and his men and officers who so zealously cooperated with him should share the praise due them." General Robert E. Lee added that he heartily agreed, and a Richmond official noted that it was "a gallant exploit, and one which exhibits what a few resolute men may do to punish the enemy on their marauding raids."

Chapter 4: The Dahlgren Papers

Back at the ambush site, the rebels looted the bodies of the slain for equipment and mementoes. One young home guardsmen, 13 year old William Littlepage, who was in a company led by their teacher, Captain Edward Halbach, was lucky enough to be the first to find Dahlgren's body. Rifling through his effects, he found a pocket watch, a cigar case, a notebook and several loose sheets of paper. Once it was light enough to read, Littlepage showed these to Halbach.

The contents shocked everyone who read them, as they had come from the body of Dahlgren himself and they detailed the raid and its movements. One document in particular stood out; it was an address written and signed by Dahlgren and intended to be read to his men. It read in part, "We hope to release the prisoners from Belle Island [Libby Prison] first and having seen them fairly started we will cross the James River into Richmond, destroying the bridges after us and exhorting the released prisoners to destroy and burn the hateful City and do not allow the Rebel Leader Davis and his traitorous crew to escape."

This was beyond the rules of civilized warfare. While both sides had burned settlements during the war, neither had done it on such a large scale. Moreover, the speech appeared to suggest that Dahlgren intended to assassinate the entire Confederate government, an unthinkable act.

If anyone had any doubts, there was another document, which while unsigned was written in the same handwriting as Dahlgren's speech, that was a list of instructions intended for one of his subordinate officers. It read in part, "The men must keep together and well in hand and once in the City it must be destroyed and Jeff Davis and Cabinet killed." The pocket notebook, which also bore Dahlgren's signature, included a draft of the speech with the same line urging his men not to let the government officials escape, plus another page with notes to himself that included the line, "Jeff Davis and Cabinet must be killed on the spot."

Captain Halbach showed the papers to his superior officer, Captain Richard Hugh Bagby. When Lieutenant James Pollard joined the group around 2 p.m., he was shown the papers. Immediately recognizing their significance, Pollard took the papers to his superior, Colonel Richard Beale, who received them that same evening. Pollard also brought along a detailed report of the ambush and Dahlgren's wooden leg as proof that the man had been killed. Beale ordered Pollard to continue to Richmond the next morning. Beale kept the notebook, thinking that it might give him information as to the location of other raiders who had not yet been captured.

Pollard reached the Confederate capital around noon of March 4 and presented the papers and wooden leg to Major General Fitzhugh Lee, nephew of Robert E. Lee. Once Lee had heard Pollard's report and examined the documents for himself, he went straight to President Davis' office.

Fitz Lee

Initially, the Confederate president appeared not to take the documents terribly seriously. Perhaps the utter failure of the raid left him unconcerned for his own safety, or perhaps it didn't occur to him that he had a propaganda coup on his hands. He told Lee to take the documents to the War Department to be filed away.

However, when the officials at the War Department saw the papers, they took them far more seriously than their president. Secretary of War James Seddon called in a group of newspaper reporters and showed them the documents. The reaction of the press can easily be imagined. Headlines across the South trumpeted this latest proof of Yankee evil. The *Richmond Whig* was a typical example, asking if the raiders were soldiers, "[o]r are they assassins, barbarians, thugs who have forfeited (and expect to lose) their lives? Are they not barbarians redolent with more hellish purposes than were the Goth, the Hun or the Saracen?"

The Southern papers soon dubbed Dahlgren "Ulric the Hun," and there were calls to execute the raiders who had been taken prisoner. General Robert E. Lee quashed this by stating that they couldn't execute a man for what he intended to do, only what he had done, and that such an act would endanger Confederate prisoners in Union prisons. "How many and better men," he asked, "have we in the enemy's hands than they have in ours?"

A clerk at the Confederate War Department recorded his own insights into the matter, pointing out that alleged war crimes in the past hadn't led to mass executions and it would be unseemly to do so now. "Retaliation for such outrages committed on others having been declined, the President and the cabinet can hardly be expected to begin with such sanguinary punishments when *their own* lives are threatened. It would be an act liable to grave criticism."

On March 6, the body of "Ulric the Hun" made it into the city he had hoped to burn. The March 8 issue of the *Richmond Whig* reported, "The body of Col. Ulric Dahlgren, killed in the swamps of King and Queen, by the 9th Va. Cavalry, was brought to the city Sunday night and laid at the York River depot during the greater part of the day yesterday, where large numbers of persons went to see it. It was in a pine box, clothed in Confederate shirt and pants, and shrouded in a Confederate blanket. The wooden leg had been removed by one of the soldiers. It was also noticeable that the little finger of the left hand had been cut off. Dahlgren was a small man, thin, pale, and with red hair and a goatee of the same color. His face wore an expression of agony." The finger had been cut off in order to take Dahlgren's jeweled ring. His finger had swollen and the ring couldn't be pried loose, so some anonymous rebel pulled out his knife and got to cutting.

After being left on display for a time, Dahlgren's body was buried in an unmarked grave in the city. Union sympathizers later snuck into the graveyard, dug it up, and reburied it outside the city. Rear Admiral Dahlgren requested that his son's remains be sent home, and they were later interred in North Hill Cemetery in Philadelphia.

It wasn't until March 8 that Kilpatrick had any firsthand accounts of what had happened. He wrote to Pleasonton, "Twelve men of Dahlgren's party have come in. They state that Colonels Dahlgren and Cooke, with about 80 men and a large number of Negroes, were ambushed at King and Queen Court-House on Thursday evening, 11 p.m. The colonel was killed and seven men wounded. Colonel [Major] Cooke and the remainder were afterward surrounded by the citizens and soldiers on furlough. Colonel [Major] Cooke ordered his men to scatter and make for the river. The Negroes were captured and confined in the jail at the court-house. Colonel Dahlgren's servant has also come in. He reports seeing the colonel's body on the roadside stripped of his clothing and horribly mutilated."

This prompted Kilpatrick to set out to avenge the death of the young colonel. In a report dated March 16 he wrote, "The outrageous treatment of the remains of Colonel Dahlgren and the cruel and barbarous manner in which his men were hunted down and captured by citizens and soldiers with dogs determined me to visit the neighborhood of King and Queen Court-House with a sufficient force to punish those who had been engaged in the murder of Colonel Dahlgren and the capture of his men. With about 2,000 cavalry, three regiments of infantry, and a battery of artillery, under command of Brigadier-General Wistar, we marched to Plymouth, near King and Queen Court-House, from which point Colonel Onderdonk, of the First New York Mounted Rifles, pushed forward to King and Queen Court-House and Carlton's Store, drove the enemy, some 1,200 strong, from his camp, destroyed the camp, and pursued him upward of ten miles, killing and wounding a large number and capturing 35 prisoners. After destroying a large amount of rebel stores collected at King and Queen Court-House, the command returned to camp without loss of a man."

Of course, this 11th hour aggressiveness would not save Kilpatrick's reputation, and in the meantime, the Confederate government continued to take advantage of the documents' propaganda value. They were photographed and copies were sent to the Confederate envoy to Europe, John Slidell, who had lithographed copies of the speech made and circulated around Europe, especially in England. Throughout the war the Confederacy had been trying to get the European powers to intervene, and the powerful Royal Navy could have easily broken the Union blockade that was strangling the Confederate economy. Copies of the photographs were also sent to Washington on March 30, with the question of whether or not Dahlgren was acting under official sanction. The next day the contents of Dahlgren's notebook hit the press, having finally been handed in by Colonel Beale.

Slidell

Naturally, General Meade found all this quite unsettling. He had never been a supporter of the raid and now it had backfired spectacularly. He ordered Kilpatrick to question the survivors of Dahlgren's unit to see if he had ever made the speech. In a letter to his wife, Meade wrote that the whole affair was "a pretty ugly piece of business."

Kilpatrick replied to Meade with a strident denial. None of Dahlgren's men, he said, had ever heard him make the objectionable speech. Kilpatrick admitted he had read the speech and approved it with a notation in red ink, but the line about burning the city and not allowing the government officials to escape had not been in the speech at that time. He claimed the Confederates must have added the line in order to make the raiders look bad. In this assertion he was already being supported by the Northern press, who insisted the papers were fake.

Meade duly responded to Lee, hinting that the papers may have been faked and that in any case, "Neither the United States Government, myself, nor General Kilpatrick authorized, sanctioned, or approved the burning of the city of Richmond and the killing of Mr. Davis and cabinet." Privately, however, Meade did not think that Dahlgren was solely to blame. He suspected that Kilpatrick was lying about the speech, and Captain John McEntee of the Bureau of Military Information, who had ridden with Dahlgren, thought that Kilpatrick had been in on the plans to devastate Richmond. McEntee was not reticent about his opinions and his superior officer, Provost Marshal Brig. Gen. Marsena Patrick, wrote of having spoken with McEntee: "He has the same opinion of Killpatrick [sic] that I have and says he managed just as all cowards do. He further says, that he thinks the papers are correct that were found upon Dahlgren, as they correspond with what D. told him."

Into this controversy plunged Dahlgren's father, Admiral John Dahlgren, who railed at the barbarous way his son's body had been treated and insisted that the papers were "a base forgery." Both he and Kilpatrick pointed out that in the lithographed European copies, the colonel's name was spelled "U. Dalhgren" rather than the correct spelling of "U. Dahlgren". Would the man misspell his own name? In addition, John Dahlgren asserted that Ulric always signed his full name and didn't use just the initial. The Confederate government replied that the orders must have been written down by one of the colonel's assistants who had misspelled Dahlgren's name. The people of the North found this explanation unconvincing.

Were the Dahlgren Papers a forgery? The controversy lasted well beyond the end of the war and in fact the matter is still in dispute, but the predominant evidence indicates that they were genuine. The matter of the misspelled name can be cleared up by looking at the photos taken of the original documents. In 1876, former Confederate General Jubal Early examined the photographs of the Dahlgren Papers. He found that the signature was on the reverse side of a page and that the ink from the front side had seeped through in several places, including on the signature. The "y" in the word "destroying" had soaked through the page onto the "hl" in Dahlgren's name, making the "h" look like an "l" and vice versa. Thus it looked like the original author had misspelled the name. The ink of the period often soaked through paper if the pen was held in one place for too long or if it had been dipped in too much ink. It is common when studying two-sided handwritten documents of that era to find such obscurations.

Early

When the photographs were touched up to make them more legible for publication, this mistake was repeated. The name being an unusual one, it was easy for it to be misread and for the mistake to make it into the lithograph and thus the European press. The original photographs, which Admiral Dahlgren did not see, show that the name was in fact spelled correctly, although it was hard to read. Researchers have further pointed out that Union officers customarily signed their name with the first initial only. It is not difficult to imagine that whatever Dahlgren did in his private correspondence, he might have adhered to common practice in official military documents.

It is also significant that no one, including Colonel Dahlgren's father, claimed the documents were not in his handwriting. Even so, could the fatal line of the speech have been forged? Could a false line have been added into a real speech verified by a real signature? Most modern historians think not. The line in question comes at the end of page one of a two-and-a-half page document. Unless Dahlgren had left that portion of the page conveniently blank, the Confederates would have had to rewrite the entire document. This is unlikely since the speech is written on Federal Cavalry Corps stationary, complete with letterhead. The notebook and separate instruction sheet would also have to be forged since they included similar lines about the fate of Richmond and its officials.

Historian Stephen Sears has pointed out that there is no way the officers in the field would have had the means to commit the forgery, so it would have to have taken place between noon on

March 4, when Pollard made it to Richmond, and early that evening, when the newspaper reporters were called in. To imagine that the plot was hatched and the forgery committed in so short of a time stretches belief to the breaking point. The plot would also have required the lifelong silence of numerous field officers and government officials who after the war would have had nothing to fear and a great deal to profit from coming clean.

The question remains, however, as to who made the fateful order. Was it purely Dahlgren's plan, or did the plot go further up the chain of command? The Southern press certainly thought it did, and some newspapers asserted that Lincoln himself gave the order. In the North, too, there was suspicion. Most of it focused on Kilpatrick, whose reputation was now thoroughly ruined thanks to his bungling of the raid. Kilpatrick claimed that he never saw the offending passage in the speech, but since the only other witness was dead, this was an easy denial to make. It is clear that for whatever reason, Dahlgren never made the speech, and Kilpatrick knew this because he had talked to Dahlgren's men himself.

Meade was so suspicious of Kilpatrick that he essentially kicked him out of the Army of the Potomac, although Kilpatrick was able to find a place under Sherman during his infamous March to the Sea. That sort of work suited him well, since it involved living off the land and burning anything in his path.

Would Kilpatrick have approved of killing the Confederate president and his cabinet? Kilpatrick had an eye on political advancement, and such a coup could certainly help it, assuming he was confident that he would find approval for it in Washington. He had long supported a harsher hand in suppressing the rebellion. He saw no need for the rules of civilized warfare, and while he did not kill unarmed civilians, officials of an enemy government were another thing entirely. They were, after all, the men who had started the war and urged their troops into battle.

Even so, it seems doubtful that he would take on such a course of action unless he had support from someone higher up. Kilpatrick had his post-war political career to think about, and while he could be impulsive on the battlefield, he was careful and methodical when it came to his long-term plans. Since Pleasonton and Meade both showed little or no support for the raid, they certainly wouldn't have approved of its more radical variant. Lincoln, too, would not have approved of such a measure; the president had ample opportunity to launch a similar raid with better preparation and leadership but never did so.

One government figure, however, stands out as a possible culprit. Secretary of War Stanton had approved the raid when he met with Kilpatrick. Indeed, his support was vital for the plan to move forward. Could Kilpatrick and Stanton have discussed the assassination of the Confederate politicians at their private meeting? It's certainly possible, although there is no hard proof.

There is, however, some strong circumstantial evidence. In November 1865, several months after the war ended, Stanton ordered Francis Lieber, the keeper of the captured Confederate records, to give him everything that had to do with the raid, including the original Dahlgren Papers. Once they were in Stanton's hands, they disappeared. There is no record of their being placed back in the archives or given to any other official. They simply vanished.

In the end, the Kilpatrick-Dahlgren raid had been a failure. It had done little damage to Richmond and its defenses, and had buoyed the spirits of its defenders by proving that the home guards could protect the capital. They had defended the city against a force superior in arms, numbers, and training, and had inflicted 340 casualties, killed or captured almost 600 horses, and captured a large amount of equipment. Kilpatrick's main force had numbered about 3,000 raiders, while they directly faced as little as 500 militia and a few dozen cavalry. The rebels had scored a stunning victory against the odds.

The great casualty among the survivors was Judson Kilpatrick. For the rest of the war he would remain a brigadier general, while more capable men were promoted to higher ranks. No one wanted him in the Army of the Potomac, and so he transferred to Major General William Tecumseh Sherman's Army of the Cumberland, where he got to use his incendiary skills in the March to the Sea. Sherman said of him, "I know that Kilpatrick is a hell of a damned fool, but I want just that sort of man to command my cavalry on this expedition."

After the war, he returned to New Jersey. He failed to get the Republican nomination for the gubernatorial election but gracefully helped the chosen candidate, Marcus Ward, get elected to the office. In return, the party appointed Kilpatrick to be Minister to Chile, a post he held until 1870. It was not a plum assignment, Chile being a minor power, and the White House was now a bitterly impossible dream. In 1880, his spirits rallied enough to run for Congress, but he was badly defeated. The party again appointed him Minister to Chile, where he died in 1881. He was subsequently interred at West Point Cemetery.

The discovery of the Dahlgren papers caused widespread anger in the South at a time when support for the war was flagging. Copies of the papers were sent to Europe in the hope that the European powers, especially the British Empire, might come in on the side of the South. Before the war, the British textile mills relied on Southern cotton. Still, British support was not forthcoming; the foreign powers had already sensed the South would lose and did not want to intervene at a time when they were consolidating their widespread empires and eyeing their neighbors with suspicion. Nor did the British Empire feel the pinch of the Union blockade for long. Their colony of Egypt proved to be a good place to grow cotton, and soon their textile mills were again running at full capacity.

What the raid and the Dahlgren papers did do was to further embitter an already divided nation. When first reporting on the scandal, the *Richmond Inquirer* said, "Decidedly, we think that these Dahlgren papers will destroy, during the rest of the war, all rosewater chivalry, and that Confederate armies will make war afar and upon the rules selected by the enemy."

Meanwhile, the Union prisoners continued to languish in Libby Prison. Lodge's prison diary mentioned the poor treatment officers captured from the raid were given. In fact, they were treated as poorly as officers who had commanded black troops.

"Friday, March 11, 1864

"This morning the rebels took the four officers of the Corps D'Afrique who are here and put them with the six officers captured of the late raiding party under Col. Dahlgreen [sic] and four Negro privates into a cell they have partitioned off from one corner of our kitchen. This cell is 14 x 20 feet. So these 14 men have just about the same room as the rest of us. They have no stove nor any convenience for cooking or even washing their faces. Their food will be cold corn bread and water. Their only means of relieving nature will be an open pail in their room which will be emptied *once a day*. . ."

Many historians have noted that the spiral into violence beyond the battlefield increased in tempo after the raid. Southern soldiers, convinced that the North would stop at nothing to destroy them, matched like with like. The war would last another year, and the civilian death toll would rise on both sides. It may not be too much of a stretch to assert that the Dahlgren Raid was one of the justifications John Wilkes Booth used to justify assassinating Abraham Lincoln.

Another item taken from Dahlgren's body would have its own curious history, albeit with less fanfare. The Colonel's wooden leg had been sent to Richmond to verify his identity. The *Richmond Examiner* reported on March 8 that it was "of most beautiful design and finish." This elegant appendage was given to Lieutenant Pollard when he lost his own leg later in the war, but he found that it didn't fit him. Artificial limbs were often custom made in order to provide a more comfortable fit and smoother walking, so Pollard gave it to a Virginia soldier named John Ballard, who used it for "nine or ten months" before Ballard decided to send it to Dahlgren's father on November 8, 1865.

By then, the war was over and the Southern Cause had been lost, but this otherwise unknown Confederate veteran decided to make a peace offering to a former enemy by giving him a memento of his fallen son.

Online Resources

Other Civil War titles by Charles River Editors

Other titles about the Dahlgren Affair on Amazon

Bibliography

Hall, James O. "The Dahlgren Papers: Fact or Fabrication," in Civil War Times Illustrated

(Nov. 1983).

Jones, J.B. A Rebel War Clerk's Diary at the Confederate States Capital. Philadelphia, PA: J.B. Lippincott & Co., 1866.

Jones, J. William. "The Kilpatrick-Dahlgren Raid against Richmond," in Southern Historical Society Papers, vol. 13.

Jones, Virgil Carrington. Eight Hours before Richmond. New York, NY: Henry Holt, 1957.

Longacre, Edward G. Mounted Raids of the Civil War. Lincoln, NE: University of Nebraska Press, 1994.

McPherson James M., "A Failed Richmond Raid and Its Consequences," in Columbiad: A Quarterly Review of the War Between the States, no. 4 (Winter 1999).

Moyer, H.P. History of the Seventeenth Regiment, Pennsylvania Volunteer Cavalry. Lebanon, PA: n.p., 1911.

Pendleton, Henry C. "The death of Colonel Dahlgren," in William and Mary College Quarterly Historical Magazine, vol. XII, no. 1 (January 1932).

Schultz, Duane. The Dahlgren Affair: Terror and Conspiracy in the Civil War. New York, NY: W.W. Norton, 1998.

Sears, Stephen W., "Raid on Richmond," in MHQ: The Quarterly Journal of Military History, vol. 11, no. 1 (Autumn 1998), 88-96.

Sears, Stephen W. Controversies & Commanders: Dispatches from the Army of the Potomac. Boston, MA: Houghton Mifflin, 1999.

Sears, Stephen W., "The Dahlgren Papers Revisited", in Columbiad: A Quarterly Review of the War Between the States, vol. 3, No. 2 (Summer 1999).

Stuart, Meriwether. "Colonel Ulric Dahlgren and Richmond's Union Underground, April 1864" in The Virginia Magazine of History and Biography, vol. 72, no. 2 (April, 1964).

Tusken, Roger. "In the Bastile of the Rebels" in Journal of the Illinois State Historical Society, vol. 56, no. 2 (Summer, 1963).

United States War Department, The War of the Rebellion: A Compilation of the Official Records of the Union and Confederate Armies (Washington D.C.: Government Printing Office, 1880-1901).

Made in the USA
Columbia, SC
16 May 2021